MEDEA

by

EURIPIDES

COMPASS CIRCLE

Medea.
Written by Euripides.
Translated by Gilbert Murray.
Current edition published by Compass Circle in 2019.

Published by Compass Circle
A Division of Garcia & Kitzinger Pty Ltd
Cover copyright ©2019 by Compass Circle.

Note:
All efforts have been made to preserve original spellings and punctuation of the original edition which may include old-fashioned English spellings of words and archaic variants.

This book is a product of its time and does not reflect the same views on race, gender, sexuality, ethnicity, and interpersonal relations as it would if it were written today.

For information contact :
information@compass-circle.com

Stronger than lover's love is lover's hate. Incurable, in each, the wounds they make

EURIPIDES

SECRET WISDOM OF THE AGES SERIES

Life presents itself, it advances in a fast way. Life indeed never stops. It never stops until the end. The most diverse questions peek and fade in our minds. Sometimes we seek for answers. Sometimes we just let time go by.

The book you have now in your hands has been waiting to be discovered by you. This book may reveal the answers to some of your questions.

Books are friends. Friends who are always by your side and who can give you great ideas, advice or just comfort your soul.

A great book can make you see things in your soul that you have not yet discovered, make you see things in your soul that you were not aware of.

Great books can change your life for the better. They can make you understand fascinating theories, give you new ideas, inspire you to undertake new challenges or to walk along new paths.

Literature Classics like the one of *Medea* are indeed a secret to many, but for those of us lucky enough to have discovered them, by one way or another, these books can enlighten us. They can open a wide range of possibilities to us. Because achieving greatness requires knowledge.

The series SECRET WISDOM OF THE AGES presented by Compass Circle try to bring you the great timeless masterpieces of literature, autobiographies and personal development,.

We welcome you to discover with us fascinating works by Nathaniel Hawthorne, Sir Arthur Conan Doyle, Edith Wharton, among others.

Introduction

The *Medea*, in spite of its background of wonder and enchantment, is not a romantic play but a tragedy of character and situation. It deals, so to speak, not with the romance itself, but with the end of the romance, a thing which is so terribly often the reverse of romantic. For all but the very highest of romances are apt to have just one flaw somewhere, and in the story of Jason and Medea the flaw was of a fatal kind.

The wildness and beauty of the Argo legend run through all Greek literature, from the mass of Corinthian lays older than our present Iliad, which later writers vaguely associate with the name of Eumêlus, to the Fourth Pythian Ode of Pindar and the beautiful Argonautica of Apollonius Rhodius. Our poet knows the wildness and the beauty; but it is not these qualities that he specially seeks. He takes them almost for granted, and pierces through them to the sheer tragedy that lies below.

Jason, son of Aeson, King of Iôlcos, in Thessaly, began his life in exile. His uncle Pelias had seized his father's kingdom, and Jason was borne away to the mountains by night and given, wrapped in a purple robe, to Chiron, the Centaur. When he reached manhood he came down to Iôlcos to demand, as Pindar tells us, his ancestral honour, and stood in the market-place, a world-famous figure, one-sandalled, with his pard-skin, his two spears and his long hair, gentle and wild and fearless, as the Wise Beast had reared him. Pelias, cowed but loath to yield, promised to give up the kingdom if Jason would make his way to the unknown land of Colchis and perform a double quest. First, if I read Pindar aright, he must fetch back the soul of his kinsman Phrixus, who had died there far from home; and, secondly, find the fleece of the Golden Ram which Phrixus had sacrificed. Jason undertook the quest: gathered the most daring heroes from all parts of Hellas; built the first ship, Argo, and set to sea. After all manner of desperate adventures he reached the land of Aiêtês, king of the Colchians, and there hope failed him. By policy, by tact, by sheer courage he did all that man could do. But Aiêtês was both hostile and treacherous. The Argonauts were surrounded, and their destruction seemed only a question of days when, suddenly, unasked, and by the mercy of Heaven, Aiêtês' daughter, Mêdêa, an enchantress as well as a princess, fell in love with Jason. She helped him through all his trials; slew for him her own sleepless serpent, who guarded the fleece; deceived her father, and secured both the fleece and the soul of Phrixus. At the last moment it appeared that her brother, Absyrtus, was about to lay an ambush for Jason. She invited Absyrtus to her room, stabbed him dead, and fled with Jason over the seas. She had given up all, and expected in return a perfect love.

And what of Jason? He could not possibly avoid taking Medea with him. He probably rather loved her. She formed at the least a brilliant addition to the glory of his enterprise. Not many heroes could produce a barbarian princess ready to leave all and follow them in blind trust. For of course, as every one knew without the telling in fifth-century Athens, no legal marriage was possible between a Greek and a barbarian from Colchis.

All through the voyage home, a world-wide baffled voyage by the Ister and the Eridanus and the African Syrtes, Medea was still in her element, and proved a constant help and counsellor to the Argonauts. When they reached Jason's home, where Pelias was still king, things began to be different. An ordered and law-abiding Greek state was scarcely the place for the untamed Colchian. We only know the catastrophe. She saw with smothered rage how Pelias hated Jason and was bent on keeping the kingdom from him, and she determined to do her lover another act of splendid service. Making the most of her fame as an enchantress, she persuaded Pelias that he could, by a certain process, regain his youth. He eagerly caught at the hope. His daughters tried the process upon him, and Pelias died in agony. Surely

Jason would be grateful now!

The real result was what it was sure to be in a civilised country. Medea and her lover had to fly for their lives, and Jason was debarred for ever from succeeding to the throne of Iôlcos. Probably there was another result also in Jason's mind: the conclusion that at all costs he must somehow separate himself from this wild beast of a woman who was ruining his life. He directed their flight to Corinth, governed at the time by a ruler of some sort, whether "tyrant" or king, who was growing old and had an only daughter. Creon would naturally want a son-in-law to support and succeed him. And where in all Greece could he find one stronger or more famous than the chief of the Argonauts? If only Medea were not there! No doubt Jason owed her a great debt for her various services. Still, after all, he was not married to her. And a man must not be weak in such matters as these. Jason accepted the princess's hand, and when Medea became violent, found it difficult to be really angry with Creon for instantly condemning her to exile. At this point the tragedy begins.

The *Medea* is one of the earliest of Euripides' works now preserved to us. And those of us who have in our time glowed at all with the religion of realism, will probably feel in it many of the qualities of youth. Not, of course, the more normal, sensuous, romantic youth, the youth of *Romeo and Juliet*; but another kind—crude, austere, passionate—the youth of the poet who is also a sceptic and a devotee of truth, who so hates the conventionally and falsely beautiful that he is apt to be unduly ascetic towards beauty itself. When a writer really deficient in poetry walks in this path, the result is purely disagreeable. It produces its best results when the writer, like Euripides or Tolstoy, is so possessed by an inward flame of poetry that it breaks out at the great moments and consumes the cramping theory that would hold it in. One can feel in the *Medea* that the natural and inevitable romance of the story is kept rigidly down. One word about Medea's ancient serpent, two or three references to the Clashing Rocks, one startling flash of light upon the real love of Jason's life, love for the ship Argo, these are almost all the concessions made to us by the merciless delineator of disaster into whose hands we are fallen. Jason is a middle-aged man, with much glory, indeed, and some illusions; but a man entirely set upon building up a great career, to whom love and all its works, though at times he has found them convenient, are for the most part only irrational and disturbing elements in a world which he can otherwise mould to his will. And yet, most cruel touch of all, one feels this man to be the real Jason. It is not that he has fallen from his heroic past. It is that he was really like this always. And so with Medea. It is not only that her beauty has begun to fade; not only that she is set in surroundings which vaguely belittle and weaken her, making her no more a bountiful princess, but only an ambiguous and much criticised foreigner. Her very devotion of love for Jason, now turned to hatred, shows itself to have been always of that somewhat rank and ugly sort to which such a change is natural.

For concentrated dramatic quality and sheer intensity of passion few plays ever written can vie with the *Medea*. Yet it obtained only a third prize at its first production; and, in spite of its immense fame, there are not many scholars who would put it among their favourite tragedies. The comparative failure of the first production was perhaps due chiefly to the extreme originality of the play. The Athenians in 432 B.C. had not yet learnt to understand or tolerate such work as this, though it is likely enough that they fortified their unfavourable opinion by the sort of criticisms which we still find attributed to Aristotle and Dicæarchus.

At the present time it is certainly not the newness of the subject: I do not think it is Aegeus, nor yet the dragon chariot, much less Medea's involuntary burst of tears in the second scene with Jason, that really produces the feeling of dissatisfaction with which many people must rise from this great play. It is rather the general scheme on which the drama is built. It is a scheme which occurs again and again in Euripides, a study of oppression and revenge. Such a subject in the hands of a more ordinary writer would probably take the form of a triumph of oppressed virtue. But Euripides gives us nothing so sympathetic, nothing so cheap and unreal. If oppression usually made people virtuous, the problems of the world would be very different from what they are. Euripides seems at times to hate the revenge of the oppressed almost as much as the original cruelty of the oppressor; or, to put the same fact in a different light, he seems deliberately to dwell upon the twofold evil of cruelty, that it not only causes pain to the victim, but actually by means of the pain makes him a worse man, so that when his turn of triumph comes, it is no longer a triumph of justice or a thing to make men rejoice. This is a grim lesson; taught often enough by history, though seldom by the fables of the poets.

Seventeen years later than the *Medea* Euripides expressed this sentiment in a more positive way in the *Trojan Women*, where a depth of wrong borne without revenge becomes, or seems for the moment to become, a thing beautiful and glorious. But more plays are constructed like the *Medea*. The *Hecuba* begins with a noble and injured Queen, and ends with her hideous vengeance on her enemy and his innocent sons. In the *Orestes* all our hearts go out to the suffering and deserted prince, till we find at last that we have committed ourselves to the blood-thirst of a madman. In the *Electra*, the workers of the vengeance themselves repent.

The dramatic effect of this kind of tragedy is curious. No one can call it undramatic or tame. Yet it is painfully unsatisfying. At the close of the *Medea* I actually find myself longing for a *deus ex machinâ*, for some being like Artemis in the *Hippolytus* or the good Dioscuri of the *Electra*, to speak a word of explanation or forgiveness, or at least leave some sound of music in our ears to drown that dreadful and insistent clamour of hate. The truth is that in this play Medea herself is the *dea ex machinâ*. The woman whom Jason and Creon intended simply to crush has been transformed by her injuries from an individual human being into a sort of living Curse. She is inspired with superhuman force. Her wrongs and her hate fill all the sky. And the judgment pronounced on Jason comes not from any disinterested or peacemaking God, but from his own victim transfigured into a devil.

From any such judgment there is an instant appeal to sane human sympathy. Jason has suffered more than enough. But that also is the way of the world. And the last word upon these tragic things is most often something not to be expressed by the sentences of even the wisest articulate judge, but only by the unspoken *lacrimæ rerum*.

G. M.

Medea of Euripides

CHARACTERS OF THE PLAY

Medea, *daughter of Aiêtês, King of Colchis.*

Jason, *chief of the Argonauts; nephew of Pelias, King of Iôlcos in Thessaly.*

Creon, *ruler of Corinth.*

Aegeus, *King of Athens.*

Nurse *of Medea.*

Two Children *of Jason and Medea.*

Attendant *on the children.*

A Messenger.

Chorus of Corinthian Women, with their Leader.
Soldiers and Attendants.

The scene is laid in Corinth. The play was first acted when Pythodôrus was Archon, Olympiad 87, year 1 (B.C. 431). Euphorion was first, Sophocles second, Euripides third, with Medea, Philoctêtes, Dictys, and the Harvesters, a Satyr-play.

Medea

The Scene represents the front of Medea's *House in Corinth.
A road to the right leads towards the royal castle, one
on the left to the harbour. The* Nurse *is discovered
alone.*

NURSE.

Would God no Argo e'er had winged the seas
To Colchis through the blue Symplêgades:
No shaft of riven pine in Pêlion's glen
Shaped that first oar-blade in the hands of men
Valiant, who won, to save King Pelias' vow,
The fleece All-golden! Never then, I trow,
Mine own princess, her spirit wounded sore
With love of Jason, to the encastled shore
Had sailed of old Iôlcos: never wrought
The daughters of King Pelias, knowing not,
To spill their father's life: nor fled in fear,
Hunted for that fierce sin, to Corinth here
With Jason and her babes. This folk at need
Stood friend to her, and she in word and deed
Served alway Jason. Surely this doth bind,
Through all ill days, the hurts of humankind,
When man and woman in one music move.

But now, the world is angry, and true love
Sick as with poison. Jason doth forsake
My mistress and his own two sons, to make
His couch in a king's chamber. He must wed:
Wed with this Creon's child, who now is head
And chief of Corinth. Wherefore sore betrayed
Medea calleth up the oath they made,
They two, and wakes the claspèd hands again,
The troth surpassing speech, and cries amain
On God in heaven to mark the end, and how
Jason hath paid his debt.

                All fasting now
And cold, her body yielded up to pain,
Her days a waste of weeping, she hath lain,
Since first she knew that he was false. Her eyes
Are lifted not; and all her visage lies
In the dust. If friends will speak, she hears no more
Than some dead rock or wave that beats the shore:
Only the white throat in a sudden shame
May writhe, and all alone she moans the name
Of father, and land, and home, forsook that day
For this man's sake, who casteth her away.
Not to be quite shut out from home . . . alas,
She knoweth now how rare a thing that was!
Methinks she hath a dread, not joy, to see
Her children near. 'Tis this that maketh me
Most tremble, lest she do I know not what.
Her heart is no light thing, and useth not

To brook much wrong. I know that woman, aye,
And dread her! Will she creep alone to die
Bleeding in that old room, where still is laid
Lord Jason's bed? She hath for that a blade
Made keen. Or slay the bridegroom and the king,
And win herself God knows what direr thing?
'Tis a fell spirit. Few, I ween, shall stir
Her hate unscathed, or lightly humble her.

Ha! 'Tis the children from their games again,
Rested and gay; and all their mother's pain
Forgotten! Young lives ever turn from gloom!

[*The* Children *and their* Attendant *come in.*

ATTENDANT.

Thou ancient treasure of my lady's room,
What mak'st thou here before the gates alone,
And alway turning on thy lips some moan
Of old mischances? Will our mistress be
Content, this long time to be left by thee?

NURSE.

Grey guard of Jason's children, a good thrall
Hath his own grief, if any hurt befall
His masters. Aye, it holds one's heart! . . .
    Meseems
I have strayed out so deep in evil dreams,
I longed to rest me here alone, and cry
Medea's wrongs to this still Earth and Sky.

ATTENDANT.

How? Are the tears yet running in her eyes?

NURSE.

'Twere good to be like thee! . . . Her sorrow lies
Scarce wakened yet, not half its perils wrought.

ATTENDANT.

Mad spirit! . . . if a man may speak his thought
Of masters mad.—And nothing in her ears
Hath sounded yet of her last cause for tears!

[*He moves towards the house, but the* Nurse *checks him.*

NURSE.

What cause, old man? . . . Nay, grudge me not
one word.

ATTENDANT.

'Tis nothing. Best forget what thou hast heard.

NURSE.

Nay, housemate, by thy beard! Hold it not hid
From me. . . . I will keep silence if thou bid.

ATTENDANT.

I heard an old man talking, where he sate
At draughts in the sun, beside the fountain gate,
And never thought of me, there standing still
Beside him. And he said, 'Twas Creon's will,
Being lord of all this land, that she be sent,
And with her her two sons, to banishment.
Maybe 'tis all false. For myself, I know
No further, and I would it were not so.

NURSE.

Jason will never bear it--his own sons
Banished,—however hot his anger runs
Against their mother!

ATTENDANT.

                    Old love burneth low
When new love wakes, men say. He is not now
Husband nor father here, nor any kin.

NURSE.

But this is ruin! New waves breaking in
To wreck us, ere we are righted from the old!

ATTENDANT.

Well, hold thy peace. Our mistress will be told
All in good time. Speak thou no word hereof.

NURSE.

My babes! What think ye of your father's love?
God curse him not, he is my master still:
But, oh, to them that loved him, 'tis an ill
Friend. . . .

ATTENDANT.

And what man on earth is different? How?
Hast thou lived all these years, and learned but now
That every man more loveth his own head
Than other men's? He dreameth of the bed
Of this new bride, and thinks not of his sons.

NURSE.

Go: run into the house, my little ones:
All will end happily! . . . Keep them apart:
Let not their mother meet them while her heart
Is darkened. Yester night I saw a flame
Stand in her eye, as though she hated them,
And would I know not what. For sure her wrath
Will never turn nor slumber, till she hath . . .
Go: and if some must suffer, may it be
Not we who love her, but some enemy!

VOICE (*within*).

Oh shame and pain: O woe is me!
Would I could die in my misery!

[*The* Children *and the* Attendant *go in.*

NURSE.

Ah, children, hark! She moves again
    Her frozen heart, her sleeping wrath.
    In, quick! And never cross her path,
Nor rouse that dark eye in its pain;

That fell sea-spirit, and the dire
    Spring of a will untaught, unbowed.
    Quick, now!—Methinks this weeping cloud
Hath in its heart some thunder-fire,

Slow gathering, that must flash ere long.
    I know not how, for ill or well,
    It turns, this uncontrollable
Tempestuous spirit, blind with wrong.

VOICE (*within*).

Have I not suffered? Doth it call
No tears? . . . Ha, ye beside the wall
Unfathered children, God hate you
As I am hated, and him, too,
    That gat you, and this house and all!

NURSE.

For pity! What have they to do,
    Babes, with their father's sin? Why call

Thy curse on these? . . . Ah, children, all
These days my bosom bleeds for you.

Rude are the wills of princes: yea,
    Prevailing alway, seldom crossed,
    On fitful winds their moods are tossed:
'Tis best men tread the equal way.

Aye, not with glory but with peace
    May the long summers find me crowned:
    For gentleness—her very sound
Is magic, and her usages.

All wholesome: but the fiercely great
    Hath little music on his road,
    And falleth, when the hand of God
Shall move, most deep and desolate.

[*During the last words the* Leader *of the Chorus has
entered. Other women follow her.*

LEADER.

    I heard a voice and a moan,
      A voice of the eastern seas:
      Hath she found not yet her ease?
        Speak, O agèd one.
    For I stood afar at the gate,
      And there came from within a cry,
    And wailing desolate.

Ah, no more joy have I,
For the griefs this house doth see,
And the love it hath wrought in me.

NURSE.

There is no house! 'Tis gone. The lord
Seeketh a prouder bed: and she
Wastes in her chamber, not one word
Will hear of care or charity.

VOICE (*within*).

O Zeus, O Earth, O Light,
Will the fire not stab my brain?
What profiteth living? Oh,
Shall I not lift the slow
Yoke, and let Life go,
As a beast out in the night,
To lie, and be rid of pain?

CHORUS.

Some Women.

A.

"O Zeus, O Earth, O Light:"
The cry of a bride forlorn
Heard ye, and wailing born
Of lost delight?

B.

Why weariest thou this day,
    Wild heart, for the bed abhorrèd,
The cold bed in the clay?
Death cometh though no man pray,
    Ungarlanded, un-adorèd.
       Call him not thou.

C.

If another's arms be now
    Where thine have been,
    On his head be the sin:
Rend not thy brow!

D.

All that thou sufferest,
  God seeth: Oh, not so sore
Waste nor weep for the breast
  That was thine of yore.

VOICE (*within*).

Virgin of Righteousness,
Virgin of hallowed Troth,
Ye marked me when with an oath
I bound him; mark no less
That oath's end. Give me to see
Him and his bride, who sought
My grief when I wronged her not,

19

Broken in misery,
And all her house. . . . O God,
My mother's home, and the dim
Shore that I left for him,
And the voice of my brother's blood. . . .

NURSE.

Oh, wild words! Did ye hear her cry
    To them that guard man's faith forsworn,
    Themis and Zeus? . . . This wrath new-born
Shall make mad workings ere it die.

CHORUS.

Other Women.

A.

Would she but come to seek
    Our faces, that love her well,
    And take to her heart the spell
        Of words that speak?

B.

Alas for the heavy hate
    And anger that burneth ever!
Would it but now abate,
Ah God, I love her yet.
    And surely my love's endeavour
        Shall fail not here.

C.

Go: from that chamber drear
   Forth to the day
Lead her, and say, Oh, say
   That we love her dear.

D.

Go, lest her hand be hard
   On the innocent: Ah, let be!
For her grief moves hitherward,
   Like an angry sea.

Nurse.

That will I: though what words of mine
Or love shall move her? Let them lie
With the old lost labours! . . . Yet her eye—
Know ye the eyes of the wild kine,

The lion flash that guards their brood?
   So looks she now if any thrall
   Speak comfort, or draw near at all
My mistress in her evil mood.

      [*The* Nurse *goes into the house.*

21

CHORUS.

A Woman.

Alas, the bold blithe bards of old
    That all for joy their music made,
For feasts and dancing manifold,
    That Life might listen and be glad.

But all the darkness and the wrong,
    Quick deaths and dim heart-aching things,
Would no man ease them with a song
    Or music of a thousand strings?

Then song had served us in our need.
    What profit, o'er the banquet's swell
That lingering cry that none may heed?
    The feast hath filled them: all is well!

OTHERS.

I heard a song, but it comes no more.
    Where the tears ran over:
A keen cry but tired, tired:
A woman's cry for her heart's desired,
    For a traitor's kiss and a lost lover.
But a prayer, methinks, yet riseth sore
    To God, to Faith, God's ancient daughter—
The Faith that over sundering seas
Drew her to Hellas, and the breeze

Of midnight shivered, and the door
  Closed of the salt unsounded water.

[*During the last words* Medea *has come out from the
house.*

MEDEA.

Women of Corinth, I am come to show
My face, lest ye despise me. For I know
Some heads stand high and fail not, even at night
Alone—far less like this, in all men's sight:
And we, who study not our wayfarings
But feel and cry—Oh we are drifting things,
And evil! For what truth is in men's eyes,
Which search no heart, but in a flash despise
A strange face, shuddering back from one that ne'er
Hath wronged them? . . . Sure, far-comers anywhere,
I know, must bow them and be gentle. Nay,
A Greek himself men praise not, who alway
Should seek his own will recking not. . . . But I—
This thing undreamed of, sudden from on high,
Hath sapped my soul: I dazzle where I stand,
The cup of all life shattered in my hand,
Longing to die—O friends! He, even he,
Whom to know well was all the world to me,
The man I loved, hath proved most evil.—Oh,
Of all things upon earth that bleed and grow,
A herb most bruised is woman. We must pay
Our store of gold, hoarded for that one day,

To buy us some man's love; and lo, they bring
A master of our flesh! There comes the sting
Of the whole shame. And then the jeopardy,
For good or ill, what shall that master be;
Reject she cannot: and if he but stays
His suit, 'tis shame on all that woman's days.
So thrown amid new laws, new places, why,
'Tis magic she must have, or prophecy—
Home never taught her that—how best to guide
Toward peace this thing that sleepeth at her side.
And she who, labouring long, shall find some way
Whereby her lord may bear with her, nor fray
His yoke too fiercely, blessed is the breath
That woman draws! Else, let her pray for death.
Her lord, if he be wearied of the face
Withindoors, gets him forth; some merrier place
Will ease his heart: but she waits on, her whole
Vision enchainèd on a single soul.
And then, forsooth, 'tis they that face the call
Of war, while we sit sheltered, hid from all
Peril!—False mocking! Sooner would I stand
Three times to face their battles, shield in hand,
Than bear one child.

                    But peace! There cannot be
Ever the same tale told of thee and me.
Thou hast this city, and thy father's home,
And joy of friends, and hope in days to come:
But I, being citiless, am cast aside

By him that wedded me, a savage bride
Won in far seas and left—no mother near,
No brother, not one kinsman anywhere
For harbour in this storm. Therefore of thee
I ask one thing. If chance yet ope to me
Some path, if even now my hand can win
Strength to requite this Jason for his sin,
Betray me not! Oh, in all things but this,
I know how full of fears a woman is,
And faint at need, and shrinking from the light
Of battle: but once spoil her of her right
In man's love, and there moves, I warn thee well,
No bloodier spirit between heaven and hell.

LEADER.

I will betray thee not. It is but just,
Thou smite him.—And that weeping in the dust
And stormy tears, how should I blame them? . . .
    Stay:
'Tis Creon, lord of Corinth, makes his way
Hither, and bears, methinks, some word of weight.

Enter from the right Creon, *the King, with armed*
Attendants.

25

CREON.

Thou woman sullen-eyed and hot with hate
Against thy lord, Medea, I here command
That thou and thy two children from this land
Go forth to banishment. Make no delay:
Seeing ourselves, the King, are come this day
To see our charge fulfilled; nor shall again
Look homeward ere we have led thy children twain
And thee beyond our realm's last boundary.

MEDEA.

Lost! Lost!
Mine haters at the helm with sail flung free
Pursuing; and for us no beach nor shore
In the endless waters! . . . Yet, though stricken sore,
I still will ask thee, for what crime, what thing
Unlawful, wilt thou cast me out, O King?

CREON.

What crime? I fear thee, woman—little need
To cloak my reasons—lest thou work some deed
Of darkness on my child. And in that fear
Reasons enough have part. Thou comest here
A wise-woman confessed, and full of lore
In unknown ways of evil. Thou art sore
In heart, being parted from thy lover's arms.
And more, thou hast made menace . . . so the alarms
But now have reached mine ear . . . on bride and

groom,
And him who gave the bride, to work thy doom
Of vengeance. Which, ere yet it be too late,
I sweep aside. I choose to earn thine hate
Of set will now, not palter with the mood
Of mercy, and hereafter weep in blood.

MEDEA.

'Tis not the first nor second time, O King,
That fame hath hurt me, and come nigh to bring
My ruin. . . . How can any man, whose eyes
Are wholesome, seek to rear his children wise
Beyond men's wont? Much helplessness in arts
Of common life, and in their townsmen's hearts
Envy deep-set . . . so much their learning brings!
Come unto fools with knowledge of new things,
They deem it vanity, not knowledge. Aye,
And men that erst for wisdom were held high,
Feel thee a thorn to fret them, privily
Held higher than they. So hath it been with me.
A wise-woman I am; and for that sin
To divers ill names men would pen me in;
A seed of strife; an eastern dreamer; one
Of brand not theirs; one hard to play upon . . .
Ah, I am not so wondrous wise!—And now,
To thee, I am terrible! What fearest thou?
What dire deed? Do I tread so proud a path—
Fear me not thou!—that I should brave the wrath
Of princes? Thou: what has thou ever done

To wrong me? Granted thine own child to one
Whom thy soul chose.—Ah, *him* out of my heart
I hate; but thou, meseems, hast done thy part
Not ill. And for thine houses' happiness
I hold no grudge. Go: marry, and God bless
Your issues. Only suffer me to rest
Somewhere within this land. Though sore oppressed,
I will be still, knowing mine own defeat.

CREON.

Thy words be gentle: but I fear me yet
Lest even now there creep some wickedness
Deep hid within thee. And for that the less
I trust thee now than ere these words began.
A woman quick of wrath, aye, or a man,
Is easier watching than the cold and still.

Up, straight, and find thy road! Mock not my will
With words. This doom is passed beyond recall;
Nor all thy crafts shall help thee, being withal
My manifest foe, to linger at my side.

Medea (*suddenly throwing herself down and clinging to*
Creon).

Oh, by thy knees! By that new-wedded bride . . .

CREON.

'Tis waste of words. Thou shalt not weaken me.

28

MEDEA.

Wilt hunt me? Spurn me when I kneel to thee?

CREON.

'Tis mine own house that kneels to me, not thou.

MEDEA.

Home, my lost home, how I desire thee now!

CREON.

And I mine, and my child, beyond all things.

MEDEA.

O Loves of man, what curse is on your wings!

CREON.

Blessing or curse, 'tis as their chances flow.

MEDEA.

Remember, Zeus, the cause of all this woe!

CREON.

Oh, rid me of my pains! Up, get thee gone!

MEDEA.

What would I with thy pains? I have mine own.

CREON.

Up: or, 'fore God, my soldiers here shall fling . . .

MEDEA.

Not that! Not that! . . . I do but pray, O King . . .

CREON.

Thou wilt not? I must face the harsher task?

MEDEA.

I accept mine exile. 'Tis not that I ask.

CREON.

Why then so wild? Why clinging to mine hand?

MEDEA (*rising*).

For one day only leave me in thy land
At peace, to find some counsel, ere the strain
Of exile fall, some comfort for these twain,
Mine innocents; since others take no thought,
It seems, to save the babes that they begot.
    Ah! Thou wilt pity them! Thou also art
A father: thou hast somewhere still a heart
That feels. . . . I reck not of myself: 'tis they
That break me, fallen upon so dire a day.

CREON.

Mine is no tyrant's mood. Aye, many a time
Ere this my tenderness hath marred the chime
Of wisest counsels. And I know that now
I do mere folly. But so be it! Thou
Shalt have this grace . . . But this I warn thee clear,
If once the morrow's sunlight find thee here
Within my borders, thee or child of thine,
Thou diest! . . . Of this judgment not a line
Shall waver nor abate. So linger on,
If thou needs must, till the next risen sun;
No further. . . . In one day there scarce can be
Those perils wrought whose dread yet haunteth me.

[*Exit* Creon *with his suite.*

CHORUS.

O woman, woman of sorrow,
　Where wilt thou turn and flee?
What town shall be thine to-morrow,
　What land of all lands that be,
What door of a strange man's home?
　Yea, God hath hunted thee,
Medea, forth to the foam
　　Of a trackless sea.

MEDEA.

Defeat on every side; what else?—But Oh,
Not here the end is: think it not! I know
For bride and groom one battle yet untried,
And goodly pains for him that gave the bride.

Dost dream I would have grovelled to this man,
Save that I won mine end, and shaped my plan
For merry deeds? My lips had never deigned
Speak word with him: my flesh been never stained
With touching. . . . Fool, Oh, triple fool! It lay
So plain for him to kill my whole essay
By exile swift: and, lo, he sets me free
This one long day: wherein mine haters three
Shall lie here dead, the father and the bride
And husband—mine, not hers! Oh, I have tried
So many thoughts of murder to my turn,
I know not which best likes me. Shall I burn
Their house with fire? Or stealing past unseen
To Jason's bed—I have a blade made keen
For that—stab, breast to breast, that wedded pair?
Good, but for one thing. When I am taken there,
And killed, they will laugh loud who hate me. . . .

Nay,

I love the old way best, the simple way
Of poison, where we too are strong as men.
Ah me!
And they being dead—what place shall hold me then?
What friend shall rise, with land inviolate

And trusty doors, to shelter from their hate
This flesh? . . . None anywhere! . . . A little more
I needs must wait: and, if there ope some door
Of refuge, some strong tower to shield me, good:
In craft and darkness I will hunt this blood.
Else, if mine hour be come and no hope nigh,
Then sword in hand, full-willed and sure to die,
I yet will live to slay them. I will wend
Man-like, their road of daring to the end.

So help me She who of all Gods hath been
The best to me, of all my chosen queen
And helpmate, Hecatê, who dwells apart,
The flame of flame, in my fire's inmost heart:
For all their strength, they shall not stab my soul
And laugh thereafter! Dark and full of dole
Their bridal feast shall be, most dark the day
They joined their hands, and hunted me away.

Awake thee now, Medea! Whatso plot
Thou hast, or cunning, strive and falter not.
On to the peril-point! Now comes the strain
Of daring. Shall they trample thee again?
How? And with Hellas laughing o'er thy fall
While this thief's daughter weds, and weds withal
Jason? . . . A true king was thy father, yea,
And born of the ancient Sun! . . . Thou know'st the
way;
And God hath made thee woman, things most vain
For help, but wondrous in the paths of pain.

[MEDEA *goes into the House.*

CHORUS.

Back streams the wave on the ever running river:
Life, life is changed and the laws of it o'ertrod.
Man shall be the slave, the affrighted, the low-liver!
　　Man hath forgotten God.
And woman, yea, woman, shall be terrible in story:
　　The tales too, meseemeth, shall be other than of
yore.
For a fear there is that cometh out of Woman and a
glory,
　　And the hard hating voices shall encompass her
no more!

The old bards shall cease, and their memory that
lingers
　　Of frail brides and faithless, shall be shrivelled as
with fire.
For they loved us not, nor knew us: and our lips were
dumb, our fingers
　　　　Could wake not the secret of the lyre.
Else, else, O God the Singer, I had sung amid their
rages
　　A long tale of Man and his deeds for good and ill.
But the old World knoweth—'tis the speech of all his
ages—
　　Man's wrong and ours: he knoweth and is still.

Some Women.

Forth from thy father's home
Thou camest, O heart of fire,
To the Dark Blue Rocks, to the clashing foam,
To the seas of thy desire:

Till the Dark Blue Bar was crossed;
And, lo, by an alien river
Standing, thy lover lost,
Void-armed for ever,

Forth yet again, O lowest
Of landless women, a ranger
Of desolate ways, thou goest,
From the walls of the stranger.

Others.

And the great Oath waxeth weak;
And Ruth, as a thing outstriven,
Is fled, fled, from the shores of the Greek,
Away on the winds of heaven.

Dark is the house afar,
Where an old king called thee daughter;
All that was once thy star
In stormy water,

Dark: and, lo, in the nearer
    House that was sworn to love thee,
Another, queenlier, dearer,
    Is thronèd above thee.

Enter from the right Jason.

JASON.

Oft have I seen, in other days than these,
How a dark temper maketh maladies
No friend can heal. 'Twas easy to have kept
Both land and home. It needed but to accept
Unstrivingly the pleasure of our lords.
But thou, for mere delight in stormy words,
Wilt lose all! . . . Now thy speech provokes not me.
Rail on. Of all mankind let Jason be
Most evil; none shall check thee. But for these
Dark threats cast out against the majesties
Of Corinth, count as veriest gain thy path
Of exile. I myself, when princely wrath
Was hot against thee, strove with all good will
To appease the wrath, and wished to keep thee still
Beside me. But thy mouth would never stay
From vanity, blaspheming night and day
Our masters. Therefore thou shalt fly the land.
    Yet, even so, I will not hold my hand
From succouring mine own people. Here am I
To help thee, woman, pondering heedfully
Thy new state. For I would not have thee flung

Provisionless away—aye, and the young
Children as well; nor lacking aught that will
Of mine can bring thee. Many a lesser ill
Hangs on the heels of exile. . . . Aye, and though
Thou hate me, dream not that my heart can know
Or fashion aught of angry will to thee.

MEDEA.

Evil, most evil! . . . since thou grantest me
That comfort, the worst weapon left me now
To smite a coward. . . . Thou comest to me, thou,
Mine enemy!

(*Turning to the* Chorus.)

Oh, say, how call ye this,
To face, and smile, the comrade whom his kiss
Betrayed? Scorn? Insult? Courage? None of these:
'Tis but of all man's inward sicknesses
The vilest, that he knoweth not of shame
Nor pity! Yet I praise him that he came . . .
To me it shall bring comfort, once to clear
My heart on thee, and thou shalt wince to hear.

I will begin with that, 'twixt me and thee,
That first befell. I saved thee. I saved thee—
Let thine own Greeks be witness, every one
That sailed on Argo—saved thee, sent alone
To yoke with yokes the bulls of fiery breath,
And sow that Acre of the Lords of Death;
And mine own ancient Serpent, who did keep

The Golden Fleece, the eyes that knew not sleep,
And shining coils, him also did I smite
Dead for thy sake, and lifted up the light
That bade thee live. Myself, uncounsellèd,
Stole forth from father and from home, and fled
Where dark Iôlcos under Pelion lies,
With thee—Oh, single-hearted more than wise!
I murdered Pelias, yea, in agony,
By his own daughters' hands, for sake of thee;
I swept their house like War.—And hast thou then
Accepted all—O evil yet again!—
And cast me off and taken thee for bride
Another? And with children at thy side!
One could forgive a childless man. But no:
I have borne thee children . . .

                 Is sworn faith so low
And weak a thing? I understand it not.
Are the old gods dead? Are the old laws forgot,
And new laws made? Since not my passioning,
But thine own heart, doth cry thee for a thing
Forsworn.

       [She catches sight of her own hand which she has
                     thrown out to denounce him.

          Poor, poor right hand of mine, whom he
Did cling to, and these knees, so cravingly,
We are unclean, thou and I; we have caught the stain
Of bad men's flesh . . . and dreamed our dreams in
vain.

38

Thou comest to befriend me? Give me, then,
Thy counsel. 'Tis not that I dream again
For good from thee: but, questioned, thou wilt show
The viler. Say: now whither shall I go?
Back to my father? Him I did betray,
And all his land, when we two fled away.
To those poor Peliad maids? For them 'twere good
To take me in, who spilled their father's blood. . . .
Aye, so my whole life stands! There were at home
Who loved me well: to them I am become
A curse. And the first friends who sheltered me,
Whom most I should have spared, to pleasure thee
I have turned to foes. Oh, therefore hast thou laid
My crown upon me, blest of many a maid
In Hellas, now I have won what all did crave,
Thee, the world-wondered lover and the brave;
Who this day looks and sees me banished, thrown
Away with these two babes, all, all, alone . . .
Oh, merry mocking when the lamps are red:
"Where go the bridegroom's babes to beg their bread
In exile, and the woman who gave all
To save him?"
               O great God, shall gold withal
Bear thy clear mark, to sift the base and fine,
And o'er man's living visage runs no sign
To show the lie within, ere all too late?

LEADER.

Dire and beyond all healing is the hate
When hearts that loved are turned to enmity.

JASON.

In speech at least, meseemeth, I must be
Not evil; but, as some old pilot goes
Furled to his sail's last edge, when danger blows
Too fiery, run before the wind and swell,
Woman, of thy loud storms.—And thus I tell
My tale. Since thou wilt build so wondrous high
Thy deeds of service in my jeopardy,
To all my crew and quest I know but one
Saviour, of Gods or mortals one alone,
The Cyprian. Oh, thou hast both brain and wit,
Yet underneath . . . nay, all the tale of it
Were graceless telling; how sheer love, a fire
Of poison-shafts, compelled thee with desire
To save me. But enough. I will not score
That count too close. 'Twas good help: and therefor
I give thee thanks, howe'er the help was wrought.
Howbeit, in my deliverance, thou hast got
Far more than given. A good Greek land hath been
Thy lasting home, not barbary. Thou hast seen
Our ordered life, and justice, and the long
Still grasp of law not changing with the strong
Man's pleasure. Then, all Hellas far and near
Hath learned thy wisdom, and in every ear

Thy fame is. Had thy days run by unseen
On that last edge of the world, where then had been
The story of great Medea? Thou and I . . .
What worth to us were treasures heapèd high
In rich kings' rooms; what worth a voice of gold
More sweet than ever rang from Orpheus old,
Unless our deeds have glory?

                              Speak I so,
Touching the Quest I wrought, thyself did throw
The challenge down. Next for thy cavilling
Of wrath at mine alliance with a king,
Here thou shalt see I both was wise, and free
From touch of passion, and a friend to thee
Most potent, and my children . . . Nay, be still!
    When first I stood in Corinth, clogged with ill
From many a desperate mischance, what bliss
Could I that day have dreamed of, like to this,
To wed with a king's daughter, I exiled
And beggared? Not—what makes thy passion wild—
From loathing of thy bed; not over-fraught
With love for this new bride; not that I sought
To upbuild mine house with offspring: 'tis enough,
What thou hast borne: I make no word thereof:
But, first and greatest, that we all might dwell
In a fair house and want not, knowing well
That poor men have no friends, but far and near
Shunning and silence. Next, I sought to rear
Our sons in nurture worthy of my race,

41

And, raising brethren to them, in one place
Join both my houses, and be all from now
Prince-like and happy. What more need hast thou
Of children? And for me, it serves my star
To link in strength the children that now are
With those that shall be.

                Have I counselled ill?
Not thine own self would say it, couldst thou still
One hour thy jealous flesh.—'Tis ever so!
Who looks for more in women? When the flow
Of love runs plain, why, all the world is fair:
But, once there fall some ill chance anywhere
To baulk that thirst, down in swift hate are trod
Men's dearest aims and noblest. Would to God
We mortals by some other seed could raise
Our fruits, and no blind women block our ways!
Then had there been no curse to wreck mankind.

LEADER.

Lord Jason, very subtly hast thou twined
Thy speech: but yet, though all athwart thy will
I speak, this is not well thou dost, but ill,
Betraying her who loved thee and was true.

MEDEA.

Surely I have my thoughts, and not a few
Have held me strange. To me it seemeth, when
A crafty tongue is given to evil men

'Tis like to wreck, not help them. Their own brain
Tempts them with lies to dare and dare again,
Till . . . no man hath enough of subtlety.
As thou—be not so seeming-fair to me
Nor deft of speech. One word will make thee fall.
Wert thou not false, 'twas thine to tell me all,
And charge me help thy marriage path, as I
Did love thee; not befool me with a lie.

JASON.

An easy task had that been! Aye, and thou
A loving aid, who canst not, even now,
Still that loud heart that surges like the tide!

MEDEA.

That moved thee not. Thine old barbarian bride,
The dog out of the east who loved thee sore,
She grew grey-haired, she served thy pride no more.

JASON.

Now understand for once! The girl to me
Is nothing, in this web of sovranty
I hold. I do but seek to save, even yet,
Thee: and for brethren to our sons beget
Young kings, to prosper all our lives again.

MEDEA.

God shelter me from prosperous days of pain,
And wealth that maketh wounds about my heart.

JASON.

Wilt change that prayer, and choose a wiser part?
Pray not to hold true sense for pain, nor rate
Thyself unhappy, being too fortunate.

MEDEA.

Aye, mock me; thou hast where to lay thine head,
But I go naked to mine exile.

JASON.

Tread
Thine own path! Thou hast made it all to be.

MEDEA.

How? By seducing and forsaking thee?

JASON.

By those vile curses on the royal halls
Let loose. . . .

MEDEA.

On thy house also, as chance falls,
I am a living curse.

JASON.

Oh, peace! Enough
Of these vain wars: I will no more thereof.

44

If thou wilt take from all that I possess
Aid for these babes and thine own helplessness
Of exile, speak thy bidding. Here I stand
Full-willed to succour thee with stintless hand,
And send my signet to old friends that dwell
On foreign shores, who will entreat thee well.
Refuse, and thou shalt do a deed most vain.
But cast thy rage away, and thou shalt gain
Much, and lose little for thine anger's sake.

MEDEA.

I will not seek thy friends. I will not take
Thy givings. Give them not. Fruits of a stem
Unholy bring no blessing after them.

JASON.

Now God in heaven be witness, all my heart
Is willing, in all ways, to do its part
For thee and for thy babes. But nothing good
Can please thee. In sheer savageness of mood
Thou drivest from thee every friend. Wherefore
I warrant thee, thy pains shall be the more.

[*He goes slowly away.*

MEDEA.

Go: thou art weary for the new delight
Thou wooest, so long tarrying out of sight
Of her sweet chamber. Go, fulfil thy pride,

45

O bridegroom! For it may be, such a bride
Shall wait thee,—yea, God heareth me in this—
As thine own heart shall sicken ere it kiss.

*   *   *   *   *   *   *   *   *   *

CHORUS.

Alas, the Love that falleth like a flood,
    Strong-winged and transitory:
Why praise ye him? What beareth he of good
    To man, or glory?
Yet Love there is that moves in gentleness,
Heart-filling, sweetest of all powers that bless.
Loose not on me, O Holder of man's heart,
    Thy golden quiver,
Nor steep in poison of desire the dart
    That heals not ever.

The pent hate of the word that cavilleth,
    The strife that hath no fill,
Where once was fondness; and the mad heart's
    breath
    For strange love panting still:
O Cyprian, cast me not on these; but sift,
Keen-eyed, of love the good and evil gift.
Make Innocence my friend, God's fairest star,
    Yea, and abate not
The rare sweet beat of bosoms without war,
    That love, and hate not.

OTHERS.

Home of my heart, land of my own,
 Cast me not, nay, for pity,
Out on my ways, helpless, alone,
Where the feet fail in the mire and stone,
 A woman without a city.
Ah, not that! Better the end:
 The green grave cover me rather,
If a break must come in the days I know,
And the skies be changed and the earth below;
For the weariest road that man may wend
 Is forth from the home of his father.

Lo, we have seen: 'tis not a song
 Sung, nor learned of another.
For whom hast thou in thy direst wrong
For comfort? Never a city strong
 To hide thee, never a brother.
Ah, but the man—cursèd be he,
 Cursèd beyond recover,
Who openeth, shattering, seal by seal,
A friend's clean heart, then turns his heel,
Deaf unto love: never in me
 Friend shall he know nor lover.

[*While* Medea *is waiting downcast, seated upon her
 door-step, there passes from the left a traveller with
 followers. As he catches sight of* Medea *he stops.*

47

AEGEUS.

Have joy, Medea! 'Tis the homeliest
Word that old friends can greet with, and the best.

MEDEA (*looking up, surprised*).

Oh, joy on thee, too, Aegeus, gentle king
Of Athens!—But whence com'st thou journeying?

AEGEUS.

From Delphi now and the old encavernèd stair. . .
.

MEDEA.

Where Earth's heart speaks in song? What mad'st
thou there?

AEGEUS.

Prayed heaven for children—the same search alway.

MEDEA.

Children? Ah God! Art childless to this day?

AEGEUS.

So God hath willed. Childless and desolate.

MEDEA.

What word did Phœbus speak, to change thy fate?

AEGEUS.

Riddles, too hard for mortal man to read.

MEDEA.

Which I may hear?

AEGEUS.

Assuredly: they need
A rarer wit.

MEDEA.

How said he?

AEGEUS.

Not to spill
Life's wine, nor seek for more. . . .

MEDEA.

Until?

AEGEUS.

Until
I tread the hearth-stone of my sires of yore.

MEDEA.

And what should bring thee here, by Creon's
shore?

AEGEUS.

One Pittheus know'st thou, high lord of Trozên?

MEDEA.

Aye, Pelops' son, a man most pure of sin.

AEGEUS.

Him I would ask, touching Apollo's will.

MEDEA.

Much use in God's ways hath he, and much skill.

AEGEUS.

And, long years back he was my battle-friend,
The truest e'er man had.

MEDEA.

              Well, may God send
Good hap to thee, and grant all thy desire.

AEGEUS.

But thou . . . ? Thy frame is wasted, and the fire
Dead in thine eyes.

MEDEA.

Aegeus, my husband is
The falsest man in the world.

AEGEUS.

What word is this?
Say clearly what thus makes thy visage dim?

MEDEA.

He is false to me, who never injured him.

AEGEUS.

What hath he done? Show all, that I may see.

MEDEA.

Ta'en him a wife; a wife, set over me
To rule his house.

AEGEUS.

He hath not dared to do,
Jason, a thing so shameful?

MEDEA.

Aye, 'tis true:
And those he loved of yore have no place now.

AEGEUS.

Some passion sweepeth him? Or is it thou
He turns from?

MEDEA.

Passion, passion to betray
His dearest!

AEGEUS.

Shame be his, so fallen away
From honour!

MEDEA.

Passion to be near a throne,
A king's heir!

AEGEUS.

How, who gives the bride? Say on.

MEDEA.

Creon, who o'er all Corinth standeth chief.

AEGEUS.

Woman, thou hast indeed much cause for grief.

MEDEA.

'Tis ruin.—And they have cast me out as well.

AEGEUS.

Who? 'Tis a new wrong this, and terrible.

MEDEA.

Creon the king, from every land and shore. . . .

AEGEUS.

And Jason suffers him? Oh, 'tis too sore!

MEDEA.

He loveth to bear bravely ills like these!
But, Aegeus, by thy beard, oh, by thy knees,
I pray thee, and I give me for thine own,
Thy suppliant, pity me! Oh, pity one
So miserable. Thou never wilt stand there
And see me cast out friendless to despair.
Give me a home in Athens . . . by the fire
Of thine own hearth! Oh, so may thy desire
Of children be fulfilled of God, and thou
Die happy! . . . Thou canst know not; even now
Thy prize is won! I, I will make of thee
A childless man no more. The seed shall be,
I swear it, sown. Such magic herbs I know.

AEGEUS.

Woman, indeed my heart goes forth to show
This help to thee, first for religion's sake,
Then for thy promised hope, to heal my ache

Of childlessness. 'Tis this hath made mine whole
Life as a shadow, and starved out my soul.
But thus it stands with me. Once make thy way
To Attic earth, I, as in law I may,
Will keep thee and befriend. But in this land,
Where Creon rules, I may not raise my hand
To shelter thee. Move of thine own essay
To seek my house, there thou shalt alway stay,
Inviolate, never to be seized again.
But come thyself from Corinth. I would fain
Even in foreign eyes be alway just.

MEDEA.

'Tis well. Give me an oath wherein to trust
And all that man could ask thou hast granted me.

AEGEUS.

Dost trust me not? Or what thing troubleth thee?

MEDEA.

I trust thee. But so many, far and near,
Do hate me—all King Pelias' house, and here
Creon. Once bound by oaths and sanctities
Thou canst not yield me up for such as these
To drag from Athens. But a spoken word,
No more, to bind thee, which no God hath heard. . .
The embassies, methinks, would come and go:
They all are friends to thee. . . . Ah me, I know

Thou wilt not list to me! So weak am I,
And they full-filled with gold and majesty.

AEGEUS.

Methinks 'tis a far foresight, this thine oath.
Still, if thou so wilt have it, nothing loath
Am I to serve thee. Mine own hand is so
The stronger, if I have this plea to show
Thy persecutors: and for thee withal
The bond more sure.—On what God shall I call?

MEDEA.

Swear by the Earth thou treadest, by the Sun,
Sire of my sires, and all the gods as one. . . .

AEGEUS.

To do what thing or not do? Make all plain.

MEDEA.

Never thyself to cast me out again.
Nor let another, whatsoe'er his plea,
Take me, while thou yet livest and art free.

AEGEUS.

Never: so hear me, Earth, and the great star
Of daylight, and all other gods that are!

MEDEA.

'Tis well: and if thou falter from thy vow . . . ?

AEGEUS.

God's judgment on the godless break my brow!

MEDEA.

Go! Go thy ways rejoicing.—All is bright
And clear before me. Go: and ere the night
Myself will follow, when the deed is done
I purpose, and the end I thirst for won.

[Aegeus *and his train depart.*

CHORUS.

Farewell: and Maia's guiding Son
Back lead thee to thy hearth and fire,
Aegeus; and all the long desire
That wasteth thee, at last be won:
Our eyes have seen thee as thou art,
A gentle and a righteous heart.

MEDEA.

God, and God's Justice, and ye blinding Skies!
At last the victory dawneth! Yea, mine eyes
See, and my foot is on the mountain's brow.
Mine enemies! Mine enemies, oh, now
Atonement cometh! Here at my worst hour

A friend is found, a very port of power
To save my shipwreck. Here will I make fast
Mine anchor, and escape them at the last
In Athens' wallèd hill.—But ere the end
'Tis meet I show thee all my counsel, friend:
Take it, no tale to make men laugh withal!

    Straightway to Jason I will send some thrall
To entreat him to my presence. Comes he here,
Then with soft reasons will I feed his ear,
How his will now is my will, how all things
Are well, touching this marriage-bed of kings
For which I am betrayed—all wise and rare
And profitable! Yet will I make one prayer,
That my two children be no more exiled
But stay. . . . Oh, not that I would leave a child
Here upon angry shores till those have laughed
Who hate me: 'tis that I will slay by craft
The king's daughter. With gifts they shall be sent,
Gifts to the bride to spare their banishment,
Fine robings and a carcanet of gold.
Which raiment let her once but take, and fold
About her, a foul death that girl shall die
And all who touch her in her agony.
Such poison shall they drink, my robe and wreath!

    Howbeit, of that no more. I gnash my teeth
Thinking on what a path my feet must tread
Thereafter. I shall lay those children dead—
Mine, whom no hand shall steal from me away!

Then, leaving Jason childless, and the day
As night above him, I will go my road
To exile, flying, flying from the blood
Of these my best-beloved, and having wrought
All horror, so but one thing reach me not,
The laugh of them that hate us.

                     Let it come!

What profits life to me? I have no home,
No country now, nor shield from any wrong.
That was my evil hour, when down the long
Halls of my father out I stole, my will
Chained by a Greek man's voice, who still, oh, still,
If God yet live, shall all requited be.
For never child of mine shall Jason see
Hereafter living, never child beget
From his new bride, who this day, desolate
Even as she made me desolate, shall die
Shrieking amid my poisons. . . . Names have I
Among your folk? One light? One weak of hand?
An eastern dreamer?—Nay, but with the brand
Of strange suns burnt, my hate, by God above,
A perilous thing, and passing sweet my love!
For these it is that make life glorious.

LEADER.

  Since thou has bared thy fell intent to us
I, loving thee, and helping in their need
Man's laws, adjure thee, dream not of this deed!

MEDEA.

There is no other way.—I pardon thee
Thy littleness, who art not wronged like me.

LEADER.

Thou canst not kill the fruit thy body bore!

MEDEA.

Yes: if the man I hate be pained the more.

LEADER.

And thou made miserable, most miserable?

MEDEA.

Oh, let it come! All words of good or ill
Are wasted now.

> [*She claps her hands: the* Nurse *comes out
> from the house.*

           Ho, woman; get thee gone
And lead lord Jason hither. . . . There is none
Like thee, to work me these high services.
But speak no word of what my purpose is,
As thou art faithful, thou, and bold to try
All succours, and a woman even as I!

> [*The* Nurse *departs.*

* * * * * * * * * *

CHORUS.

The sons of Erechtheus, the olden,
    Whom high gods planted of yore
In an old land of heaven upholden,
    A proud land untrodden of war:
They are hungered, and, lo, their desire
    With wisdom is fed as with meat:
In their skies is a shining of fire,
    A joy in the fall of their feet:
And thither, with manifold dowers,
    From the North, from the hills, from the morn,
The Muses did gather their powers,
    That a child of the Nine should be born;
And Harmony, sown as the flowers,
    Grew gold in the acres of corn.

And Cephîsus, the fair-flowing river—
    The Cyprian dipping her hand
Hath drawn of his dew, and the shiver
    Of her touch is as joy in the land.
For her breathing in fragrance is written,
    And in music her path as she goes,
And the cloud of her hair, it is litten
    With stars of the wind-woven rose.
So fareth she ever and ever,
    And forth of her bosom is blown,

As dews on the winds of the river,
   An hunger of passions unknown.
Strong Loves of all godlike endeavour,
   Whom Wisdom shall throne on her throne.

Some Women.

 But Cephîsus the fair-flowing,
Will he bear thee on his shore?
   Shall the land that succours all, succour thee,
Who art foul among thy kind,
With the tears of children blind?
Dost thou see the red gash growing,
    Thine own burden dost thou see?
      Every side, Every way,
   Lo, we kneel to thee and pray:
  By thy knees, by thy soul, O woman wild!
  One at least thou canst not slay,
     Not thy child!

Others.

 Hast thou ice that thou shalt bind it
To thy breast, and make thee dead
   To thy children, to thine own spirit's pain?
When the hand knows what it dares,
When thine eyes look into theirs,
Shalt thou keep by tears unblinded
    Thy dividing of the slain?
     These be deeds Not for thee:

These be things that cannot be!
　　Thy babes—though thine hardihood be fell,
　When they cling about thy knee,
　　　'Twill be well!

Enter Jason.

Jason.

I answer to thy call. Though full of hate
Thou be, I yet will not so far abate
My kindness for thee, nor refuse mine ear.
Say in what new desire thou hast called me here.

Medea.

Jason, I pray thee, for my words but now
Spoken, forgive me. My bad moods. . . . Oh, thou
At least wilt strive to bear with them! There be
Many old deeds of love 'twixt me and thee.
Lo, I have reasoned with myself apart
And chidden: "Why must I be mad, O heart
Of mine: and raging against one whose word
Is wisdom: making me a thing abhorred
To them that rule the land, and to mine own
Husband, who doth but that which, being done,
Will help us all—to wed a queen, and get
Young kings for brethren to my sons? And yet
I rage alone, and cannot quit my rage—
What aileth me?—when God sends harbourage
So simple? Have I not my children? Know

I not we are but exiles, and must go
Beggared and friendless else?" Thought upon thought
So pressed me, till I knew myself full-fraught
With bitterness of heart and blinded eyes.
So now—I give thee thanks: and hold thee wise
To have caught this anchor for our aid. The fool
Was I; who should have been thy friend, thy tool;
Gone wooing with thee, stood at thy bed-side
Serving, and welcomed duteously thy bride.
But, as we are, we are—I will not say
Mere evil—women! Why must thou to-day
Turn strange, and make thee like some evil thing,
Childish, to meet my childish passioning?
See, I surrender: and confess that then
I had bad thoughts, but now have turned again
And found my wiser mind.

[*She claps her hands.*

Ho, children! Run
Quickly! Come hither, out into the sun,

[*The* Children *come from the house, followed
by their* Attendant.

And greet your father. Welcome him with us,
And throw quite, quite away, as mother does,
Your anger against one so dear. Our peace
Is made, and all the old bad war shall cease
For ever.—Go, and take his hand. . . .

[*As the* Children *go to* Jason, *she suddenly
bursts into tears. The* Children *quickly
return to her: she recovers herself, smiling
amid her tears.*

Ah me,

I am full of hidden horrors! . . . Shall it be
A long time more, my children, that ye live
To reach to me those dear, dear arms? . . . Forgive!
I am so ready with my tears to-day,
And full of dread. . . . I sought to smooth away
The long strife with your father, and, lo, now
I have all drowned with tears this little brow!

[*She wipes the child's face.*

LEADER.

O'er mine eyes too there stealeth a pale tear:
Let the evil rest, O God, let it rest here!

JASON.

Woman, indeed I praise thee now, nor say
Ill of thine other hour. 'Tis nature's way,
A woman needs must stir herself to wrath,
When work of marriage by so strange a path
Crosseth her lord. But thou, thine heart doth wend
The happier road. Thou hast seen, ere quite the end,
What choice must needs be stronger: which to do
Shows a wise-minded woman. . . . And for you,

Children; your father never has forgot
Your needs. If God but help him, he hath wrought
A strong deliverance for your weakness. Yea,
I think you, with your brethren, yet one day
Shall be the mightiest voices in this land.
Do you grow tall and strong. Your father's hand
Guideth all else, and whatso power divine
Hath alway helped him. . . . Ah, may it be mine
To see you yet in manhood, stern of brow,
Strong-armed, set high o'er those that hate me. . . .

                                      How?
Woman, thy face is turned. Thy cheek is swept
With pallor of strange tears. Dost not accept
Gladly and of good will my benisons?

MEDEA.

'Tis nothing. Thinking of these little ones. . . .

JASON.

Take heart, then. I will guard them from all ill.

MEDEA.

I do take heart. Thy word I never will
Mistrust. Alas, a woman's bosom bears
But woman's courage, a thing born for tears.

JASON.

What ails thee?—All too sore thou weepest there.

MEDEA.

I was their mother! When I heard thy prayer
Of long life for them, there swept over me
A horror, wondering how these things shall be.
  But for the matter of my need that thou
Should speak with me, part I have said, and now
Will finish.—Seeing it is the king's behest
To cast me out from Corinth . . . aye, and best,
Far best, for me—I know it—not to stay
Longer to trouble thee and those who sway
The realm, being held to all their house a foe. . . .
Behold, I spread my sails, and meekly go
To exile. But our children. . . . Could this land
Be still their home awhile: could thine own hand
But guide their boyhood. . . . Seek the king, and pray
His pity, that he bid thy children stay!

JASON.

He is hard to move. Yet surely 'twere well done.

MEDEA.

Bid her—for thy sake, for a daughters boon. . . .

JASON.

Well thought! Her I can fashion to my mind.

MEDEA.

Surely. She is a woman like her kind. . . .
Yet I will aid thee in thy labour; I
Will send her gifts, the fairest gifts that lie
In the hands of men, things of the days of old,
Fine robings and a carcanet of gold,
By the boys' hands.—Go, quick, some handmaiden,
And fetch the raiment.

[*A handmaid goes into the house.*

Ah, her cup shall then
Be filled indeed! What more should woman crave,
Being wed with thee, the bravest of the brave,
And girt with raiment which of old the sire
Of all my house, the Sun, gave, steeped in fire,
To his own fiery race?

[*The handmaid has returned bearing the Gifts.*

Come, children, lift
With heed these caskets. Bear them as your gift
To her, being bride and princess and of right
Blessed!—I think she will not hold them light.

JASON.

Fond woman, why wilt empty thus thine hand
Of treasure? Doth King Creon's castle stand
In stint of raiment, or in stint of gold?
Keep these, and make no gift. For if she hold

Jason of any worth at all, I swear
Chattels like these will not weigh more with her.

MEDEA.

Ah, chide me not! 'Tis written, gifts persuade
The gods in heaven; and gold is stronger made
Than words innumerable to bend men's ways.
Fortune is hers. God maketh great her days:
Young and a crownèd queen! And banishment
For those two babes. . . . I would not gold were spent,
But life's blood, ere that come.

                             My children, go
Forth into those rich halls, and, bowing low,
Beseech your father's bride, whom I obey,
Ye be not, of her mercy, cast away
Exiled: and give the caskets—above all
Mark this!—to none but her, to hold withal
And keep. . . . Go quick! And let your mother know
Soon the good tiding that she longs for. . . . Go!

[*She goes quickly into the house.* Jason *and the* Children
with their Attendant *depart.*

*   *   *   *   *   *   *   *   *   *

CHORUS.

Now I have no hope more of the children's living;
   No hope more. They are gone forth unto death.
The bride, she taketh the poison of their giving:
   She taketh the bounden gold and openeth;
And the crown, the crown, she lifteth about her brow,
Where the light brown curls are clustering. No hope
now!

O sweet and cloudy gleam of the garments golden!
   The robe, it hath clasped her breast and the crown
her head.
Then, then, she decketh the bride, as a bride of olden
   Story, that goeth pale to the kiss of the dead.
For the ring hath closed, and the portion of death is
there;
And she flieth not, but perisheth unaware.

Some Women.

O bridegroom, bridegroom of the kiss so cold,
Art thou wed with princes, art thou girt with gold,
     Who know'st not, suing
     For thy child's undoing,
  And, on her thou lovest, for a doom untold?
How art thou fallen from thy place of old!

Others.

O Mother, Mother, what hast thou to reap,
When the harvest cometh, between wake and sleep?

For a heart unslaken,
For a troth forsaken,
Lo, babes that call thee from a bloody deep:
And thy love returns not. Get thee forth and weep!

[*Enter the* Attendant *with the two* Children: Medea
comes out from the house.

ATTENDANT.

Mistress, these children from their banishment
Are spared. The royal bride hath mildly bent
Her hand to accept thy gifts, and all is now
Peace for the children.—Ha, why standest thou
Confounded, when good fortune draweth near?

MEDEA.

Ah God!

ATTENDANT.

This chimes not with the news I bear.

MEDEA.

O God, have mercy!

ATTENDANT.

Is some word of wrath
Here hidden that I knew not of? And hath
My hope to give thee joy so cheated me?

MEDEA.

Thou givest what thou givest: I blame not thee.

ATTENDANT.

Thy brows are all o'ercast: thine eyes are filled. . .
.

MEDEA.

For bitter need, Old Man! The gods have willed,
And my own evil mind, that this should come.

ATTENDANT.

Take heart! Thy sons one day will bring thee
home.

MEDEA.

Home? . . . I have others to send home. Woe's me!

ATTENDANT.

Be patient. Many a mother before thee
Hath parted from her children. We poor things
Of men must needs endure what fortune brings.

MEDEA.

I will endure.—Go thou within, and lay
All ready that my sons may need to-day.

[*The* Attendant *goes into the house.*

O children, children mine: and you have found
A land and home, where, leaving me discrowned
And desolate, forever you will stay,
Motherless children! And I go my way
To other lands, an exile, ere you bring
Your fruits home, ere I see you prospering
Or know your brides, or deck the bridal bed,
All flowers, and lift your torches overhead.

   Oh cursèd be mine own hard heart! 'Twas all
In vain, then, that I reared you up, so tall
And fair; in vain I bore you, and was torn
With those long pitiless pains, when you were born.
Ah, wondrous hopes my poor heart had in you,
How you would tend me in mine age, and do
The shroud about me with your own dear hands,
When I lay cold, blessèd in all the lands
That knew us. And that gentle thought is dead!
You go, and I live on, to eat the bread
Of long years, to myself most full of pain.
And never your dear eyes, never again,
Shall see your mother, far away being thrown
To other shapes of life. . . . My babes, my own,
Why gaze ye so?—What is it that ye see?—
And laugh with that last laughter? . . . Woe is me,
What shall I do?

           Women, my strength is gone,
Gone like a dream, since once I looked upon

Those shining faces. . . . I can do it not.
Good-bye to all the thoughts that burned so hot
Aforetime! I will take and hide them far,
Far, from men's eyes. Why should I seek a war
So blind: by these babes' wounds to sting again
Their father's heart, and win myself a pain
Twice deeper? Never, never! I forget
Henceforward all I laboured for.

                              And yet,
What is it with me? Would I be a thing
Mocked at, and leave mine enemies to sting
Unsmitten? It must be. O coward heart,
Ever to harbour such soft words!—Depart
Out of my sight, ye twain.

                    [*The* Children *go in.*

                         And they whose eyes
Shall hold it sin to share my sacrifice,
On their heads be it! My hand shall swerve not now.

    Ah, Ah, thou Wrath within me! Do not thou,
Do not. . . . Down, down, thou tortured thing, and
spare
My children! They will dwell with us, aye, there
Far off, and give thee peace.

                         Too late, too late!
By all Hell's living agonies of hate,
They shall not take my little ones alive
To make their mock with! Howsoe'er I strive

73

The thing is doomed; it shall not escape now
From being. Aye, the crown is on the brow,
And the robe girt, and in the robe that high
Queen dying.

                I know all. Yet . . . seeing that I
Must go so long a journey, and these twain
A longer yet and darker, I would fain
Speak with them, ere I go.

             [*A handmaid brings the* Children *out again.*

                Come, children; stand
A little from me. There. Reach out your hand,
Your right hand—so—to mother: and good-bye!

        [*She has kept them hitherto at arm's length: but
             at the touch of their hands, her resolution
             breaks down, and she gathers them passionately
                       into her arms.*

Oh, darling hand! Oh, darling mouth, and eye,
And royal mien, and bright brave faces clear,
May you be blessèd, but not here! What here
Was yours, your father stole. . . . Ah God, the glow
Of cheek on cheek, the tender touch; and Oh,
Sweet scent of childhood. . . . Go! Go! . . . Am I
blind? . . .
Mine eyes can see not, when I look to find
Their places. I am broken by the wings
Of evil. . . . Yea, I know to what bad things

I go, but louder than all thought doth cry
Anger, which maketh man's worst misery.

[*She follows the* Children *into the house.*

CHORUS.

My thoughts have roamed a cloudy land,
And heard a fierier music fall
Than woman's heart should stir withal:
And yet some Muse majestical,
Unknown, hath hold of woman's hand,
Seeking for Wisdom—not in all:
A feeble seed, a scattered band,
Thou yet shalt find in lonely places,
Not dead amongst us, nor our faces
Turned alway from the Muses' call.

And thus my thought would speak: that she
Who ne'er hath borne a child nor known
Is nearer to felicity:
Unlit she goeth and alone,
With little understanding what
A child's touch means of joy or woe,
And many toils she beareth not.

But they within whose garden fair
That gentle plant hath blown, they go
Deep-written all their days with care—
To rear the children, to make fast

Their hold, to win them wealth; and then
Much darkness, if the seed at last
Bear fruit in good or evil men!
And one thing at the end of all
Abideth, that which all men dread:
The wealth is won, the limbs are bred
To manhood, and the heart withal
Honest: and, lo, where Fortune smiled,
Some change, and what hath fallen? Hark!
'Tis death slow winging to the dark,
And in his arms what was thy child.

What therefore doth it bring of gain
To man, whose cup stood full before,
That God should send this one thing more
Of hunger and of dread, a door
Set wide to every wind of pain?

[Medea *comes out alone from the house.*

MEDEA.

Friends, this long hour I wait on Fortune's eyes,
And strain my senses in a hot surmise
What passeth on that hill.—Ha! even now
There comes . . . 'tis one of Jason's men, I trow.
His wild-perturbèd breath doth warrant me
The tidings of some strange calamity.

[*Enter* Messenger.

76

MESSENGER.

O dire and ghastly deed! Get thee away,
Medea! Fly! Nor let behind thee stay
One chariot's wing, one keel that sweeps the seas. . . .

MEDEA.

And what hath chanced, to cause such flights as
these?

MESSENGER.

The maiden princess lieth—and her sire,
The king—both murdered by thy poison-fire.

MEDEA.

Most happy tiding! Which thy name prefers
Henceforth among my friends and well-wishers.

MESSENGER.

What say'st thou? Woman, is thy mind within
Clear, and not raving? Thou art found in sin
Most bloody wrought against the king's high head,
And laughest at the tale, and hast no dread?

MEDEA.

I have words also that could answer well
Thy word. But take thine ease, good friend, and tell,
How died they? Hath it been a very foul
Death, prithee? That were comfort to my soul.

MESSENGER.

When thy two children, hand in hand entwined,
Came with their father, and passed on to find
The new-made bridal rooms, Oh, we were glad,
We thralls, who ever loved thee well, and had
Grief in thy grief. And straight there passed a word
From ear to ear, that thou and thy false lord
Had poured peace offering upon wrath foregone.
A right glad welcome gave we them, and one
Kissed the small hand, and one the shining hair:
Myself, for very joy, I followed where
The women's rooms are. There our mistress . . . she
Whom now we name so . . . thinking not to see
Thy little pair, with glad and eager brow
Sate waiting Jason. Then she saw, and slow
Shrouded her eyes, and backward turned again,
Sick that thy children should come near her. Then
Thy husband quick went forward, to entreat
The young maid's fitful wrath. "Thou will not meet
Love's coming with unkindness? Nay, refrain
Thy suddenness, and turn thy face again,
Holding as friends all that to me are dear,
Thine husband. And accept these robes they bear
As gifts: and beg thy father to unmake
His doom of exile on them—for my sake."
When once she saw the raiment, she could still
Her joy no more, but gave him all his will.
And almost ere the father and the two

Children were gone from out the room, she drew
The flowerèd garments forth, and sate her down
To her arraying: bound the golden crown
Through her long curls, and in a mirror fair
Arranged their separate clusters, smiling there
At the dead self that faced her. Then aside
She pushed her seat, and paced those chambers wide
Alone, her white foot poising delicately—
So passing joyful in those gifts was she!—
And many a time would pause, straight-limbed, and wheel
Her head to watch the long fold to her heel
Sweeping. And then came something strange. Her cheek
Seemed pale, and back with crooked steps and weak
Groping of arms she walked, and scarcely found
Her old seat, that she fell not to the ground.

    Among the handmaids was a woman old
And grey, who deemed, I think, that Pan had hold
Upon her, or some spirit, and raised a keen
Awakening shout; till through her lips was seen
A white foam crawling, and her eyeballs back
Twisted, and all her face dead pale for lack
Of life: and while that old dame called, the cry
Turned strangely to its opposite, to die
Sobbing. Oh, swiftly then one woman flew
To seek her father's rooms, one for the new
Bridegroom, to tell the tale. And all the place

Was loud with hurrying feet.

      So long a space
As a swift walker on a measured way
Would pace a furlong's course in, there she lay
Speechless, with veilèd lids. Then wide her eyes
She oped, and wildly, as she strove to rise,
Shrieked: for two diverse waves upon her rolled
Of stabbing death. The carcanet of gold
That gripped her brow was molten in a dire
And wondrous river of devouring fire.
And those fine robes, the gift thy children gave—
God's mercy!—everywhere did lap and lave
The delicate flesh; till up she sprang, and fled,
A fiery pillar, shaking locks and head
This way and that, seeking to cast the crown
Somewhere away. But like a thing nailed down
The burning gold held fast the anadem,
And through her locks, the more she scattered them,
Came fire the fiercer, till to earth she fell
A thing—save to her sire—scarce nameable,
And strove no more. That cheek of royal mien,
Where was it—or the place where eyes had been?
Only from crown and temples came faint blood
Shot through with fire. The very flesh, it stood
Out from the bones, as from a wounded pine
The gum starts, where those gnawing poisons fine
Bit in the dark—a ghastly sight! And touch
The dead we durst not. We had seen too much.

But that poor father, knowing not, had sped,
Swift to his daughter's room, and there the dead
Lay at his feet. He knelt, and groaning low,
Folded her in his arms, and kissed her: "Oh,
Unhappy child, what thing unnatural hath
So hideously undone thee? Or what wrath
Of gods, to make this old grey sepulchre
Childless of thee? Would God but lay me there
To die with thee, my daughter!" So he cried.
But after, when he stayed from tears, and tried
To uplift his old bent frame, lo, in the folds
Of those fine robes it held, as ivy holds
Strangling among your laurel boughs. Oh, then
A ghastly struggle came! Again, again,
Up on his knee he writhed; but that dead breast
Clung still to his: till, wild, like one possessed,
He dragged himself half free; and, lo, the live
Flesh parted; and he laid him down to strive
No more with death, but perish; for the deep
Had risen above his soul. And there they sleep,
At last, the old proud father and the bride,
Even as his tears had craved it, side by side.

   For thee—Oh, no word more! Thyself will know
How best to baffle vengeance. . . . Long ago
I looked upon man's days, and found a grey
Shadow. And this thing more I surely say,
That those of all men who are counted wise,
Strong wits, devisers of great policies,

Do pay the bitterest toll. Since life began,
Hath there in God's eye stood one happy man?
Fair days roll on, and bear more gifts or less
Of fortune, but to no man happiness.

[*Exit* Messenger.

CHORUS.

Some Women.

Wrath upon wrath, meseems, this day shall fall
From God on Jason! He hath earned it all.

Other Women.

O miserable maiden, all my heart
Is torn for thee, so sudden to depart
From thy king's chambers and the light above
To darkness, all for sake of Jason's love!

MEDEA.

Women, my mind is clear. I go to slay
My children with all speed, and then, away
From hence; not wait yet longer till they stand
Beneath another and an angrier hand
To die. Yea, howsoe'er I shield them, die
They must. And, seeing that they must, 'tis I
Shall slay them, I their mother, touched of none
Beside. Oh, up and get thine armour on,
My heart! Why longer tarry we to win

Our crown of dire inevitable sin?
Take up thy sword, O poor right hand of mine,
Thy sword: then onward to the thin-drawn line
Where life turns agony. Let there be naught
Of softness now: and keep thee from that thought,
'Born of thy flesh,' 'thine own belovèd.' Now,
For one brief day, forget thy children: thou
Shalt weep hereafter. Though thou slay them, yet
Sweet were they. . . . I am sore unfortunate.

[*She goes into the house.*

CHORUS.

Some Women.

O Earth, our mother; and thou
  All-seër, arrowy crown
Of Sunlight, manward now
  Look down, Oh, look down!
Look upon one accurst,
  Ere yet in blood she twine
  Red hands—blood that is thine!
O Sun, save her first!
She is thy daughter still,
  Of thine own golden line;
Save her! Or shall man spill
  The life divine?
Give peace, O Fire that diest not! Send thy spell
  To stay her yet, to lift her afar, afar—

A torture-changèd spirit, a voice of Hell
  Wrought of old wrongs and war!

Others.

  Alas for the mother's pain
    Wasted! Alas the dear
  Life that was born in vain!
    Woman, what mak'st thou here,
  Thou from beyond the Gate
    Where dim Symplêgades
    Clash in the dark blue seas,
  The shores where death doth wait?
  Why hast thou taken on thee,
    To make us desolate,
  This anger of misery
    And guilt of hate?
For fierce are the smitings back of blood once shed
  Where love hath been: God's wrath upon them
that kill,
And an anguished earth, and the wonder of the dead
    Haunting as music still. . . .

                    [*A cry is heard within.*

A Woman.

Hark! Did ye hear? Heard ye the children's cry?

Another.

O miserable woman! O abhorred!

A Child within.

What shall I do? What is it? Keep me fast
From mother!

The Other Child.

        I know nothing. Brother! Oh,
I think she means to kill us.

A Woman.

          Let me go!
I will—Help! Help!—and save them at the last.

A Child.

Yes, in God's name! Help quickly ere we die!

The Other Child.

She has almost caught me now. She has a sword.

[*Many of the Women are now beating at the barred door
to get in. Others are standing apart.*

Women at the door.

Thou stone, thou thing of iron! Wilt verily
Spill with thine hand that life, the vintage stored
Of thine own agony?

The Other Women.

A Mother slew her babes in days of yore,
One, only one, from dawn to eventide,
  Ino, god-maddened, whom the Queen of
    Heaven
    Set frenzied, flying to the dark: and she
    Cast her for sorrow to the wide salt sea,
  Forth from those rooms of murder unforgiven,
Wild-footed from a white crag of the shore,
  And clasping still her children twain, she died.

O Love of Woman, charged with sorrow sore,
  What hast thou wrought upon us? What beside
    Resteth to tremble for?

[*Enter hurriedly* Jason *and Attendants.*

JASON.

Ye women by this doorway clustering
Speak, is the doer of the ghastly thing
Yet here, or fled? What hopeth she of flight?
Shall the deep yawn to shield her? Shall the height
Send wings, and hide her in the vaulted sky
To work red murder on her lords, and fly
Unrecompensed? But let her go! My care
Is but to save my children, not for her.
Let them she wronged requite her as they may.
I care not. 'Tis my sons I must some way

86

Save, ere the kinsmen of the dead can win
From them the payment of their mother's sin.

LEADER.

Unhappy man, indeed thou knowest not
What dark place thou art come to! Else, God wot,
Jason, no word like these could fall from thee.

JASON.

What is it?—Ha! The woman would kill me?

LEADER.

Thy sons are dead, slain by their mother's hand.

JASON.

How? Not the children. . . . I scarce understand. . .
.
O God, thou hast broken me!

LEADER.

                             Think of those twain
As things once fair, that ne'er shall bloom again.

JASON.

Where did she murder them? In that old room?

LEADER.

Open, and thou shalt see thy children's doom.

JASON.

Ho, thralls! Unloose me yonder bars! Make more
Of speed! Wrench out the jointing of the door.
And show my two-edged curse, the children dead,
The woman. . . . Oh, this sword upon her head. . . .

[*While the Attendants are still battering at the door*
Medea *appears on the roof, standing on a chariot of*
winged Dragons, in which are the children's bodies.

MEDEA.

What make ye at my gates? Why batter ye
With brazen bars, seeking the dead and me
Who slew them? Peace! . . . And thou, if aught of
mine
Thou needest, speak, though never touch of thine
Shall scathe me more. Out of his firmament
My fathers' father, the high Sun, hath sent
This, that shall save me from mine enemies' rage.

JASON.

Thou living hate! Thou wife in every age
Abhorrèd, blood-red mother, who didst kill
My sons, and make me as the dead: and still
Canst take the sunshine to thine eyes, and smell
The green earth, reeking from thy deed of hell;
I curse thee! Now, Oh, now mine eyes can see,
That then were blinded, when from savagery

Of eastern chambers, from a cruel land,
To Greece and home I gathered in mine hand
Thee, thou incarnate curse: one that betrayed
Her home, her father, her . . . Oh, God hath laid
Thy sins on me!—I knew, I knew, there lay
A brother murdered on thy hearth that day
When thy first footstep fell on Argo's hull. . . .
Argo, my own, my swift and beautiful

    That was her first beginning. Then a wife
I made her in my house. She bore to life
Children: and now for love, for chambering
And men's arms, she hath murdered them! A thing
Not one of all the maids of Greece, not one,
Had dreamed of; whom I spurned, and for mine own
Chose thee, a bride of hate to me and death,
Tigress, not woman, beast of wilder breath
Than Skylla shrieking o'er the Tuscan sea.
Enough! No scorn of mine can reach to thee,
Such iron is o'er thine eyes. Out from my road,
Thou crime-begetter, blind with children's blood!
And let me weep alone the bitter tide
That sweepeth Jason's days, no gentle bride
To speak with more, no child to look upon
Whom once I reared . . . all, all for ever gone!

MEDEA.

    An easy answer had I to this swell
Of speech, but Zeus our father knoweth well,
All I for thee have wrought, and thou for me.

So let it rest. This thing was not to be,
That thou shouldst live a merry life, my bed
Forgotten and my heart uncomforted,
Thou nor thy princess: nor the king that planned
Thy marriage drive Medea from his land,
And suffer not. Call me what thing thou please,
Tigress or Skylla from the Tuscan seas:
My claws have gripped thine heart, and all things
shine.

JASON.

Thou too hast grief. Thy pain is fierce as mine.

MEDEA.

I love the pain, so thou shalt laugh no more.

JASON.

Oh, what a womb of sin my children bore!

MEDEA.

Sons, did ye perish for your father's shame?

JASON.

How? It was not my hand that murdered them.

MEDEA.

'Twas thy false wooings, 'twas thy trampling pride.

JASON.

Thou hast said it! For thy lust of love they died.

MEDEA.

And love to women a slight thing should be?

JASON.

To women pure!—All thy vile life to thee!

MEDEA.

Think of thy torment. They are dead, they are dead!

JASON.

No: quick, great God; quick curses round thy head!

MEDEA.

The Gods know who began this work of woe.

JASON.

Thy heart and all its loathliness they know.

MEDEA.

Loathe on. . . . But, Oh, thy voice. It hurts me sore.

JASON.

Aye, and thine me. Wouldst hear me then no more?

MEDEA.

How? Show me but the way. 'Tis this I crave.

JASON.

Give me the dead to weep, and make their grave.

MEDEA.

Never! Myself will lay them in a still
Green sepulchre, where Hera by the Hill
Hath precinct holy, that no angry men
May break their graves and cast them forth again
To evil. So I lay on all this shore
Of Corinth a high feast for evermore
And rite, to purge them yearly of the stain
Of this poor blood. And I, to Pallas' plain
I go, to dwell beside Pandion's son,

AEGEUS.

—For thee, behold, death draweth on,
Evil and lonely, like thine heart: the hands
Of thine old Argo, rotting where she stands,
Shall smite thine head in twain, and bitter be
To the last end thy memories of me.

[*She rises on the chariot and is slowly borne away.*

JASON.

May They that hear the weeping child
Blast thee, and They that walk in blood!

MEDEA.

Thy broken vows, thy friends beguiled
Have shut for thee the ears of God.

JASON.

Go, thou art wet with children's tears!

MEDEA.

Go thou, and lay thy bride to sleep.

JASON.

Childless, I go, to weep and weep.

MEDEA.

Not yet! Age cometh and long years.

JASON.

My sons, mine own!

MEDEA.

Not thine, but mine . . .

JASON.

. . . Who slew them!

MEDEA.

Yes: to torture thee.

JASON.

Once let me kiss their lips, once twine
Mine arms and touch. . . . Ah, woe is me!

MEDEA.

Wouldst love them and entreat? But now
They were as nothing.

JASON.

At the last,
O God, to touch that tender brow!

MEDEA.

Thy words upon the wind are cast.

JASON.

Thou, Zeus, wilt hear me. All is said
For naught. I am but spurned away
And trampled by this tigress, red
With children's blood. Yet, come what may,
So far as thou hast granted, yea,

So far as yet my strength may stand,
I weep upon these dead, and say
   Their last farewell, and raise my hand

To all the daemons of the air
   In witness of these things; how she
   Who slew them, will not suffer me
To gather up my babes, nor bear
To earth their bodies; whom, O stone
Of women, would I ne'er had known
   Nor gotten, to be slain by thee!

       [*He casts himself upon the earth.*

CHORUS.

Great treasure halls hath Zeus in heaven,
  From whence to man strange dooms be given,
      Past hope or fear.
And the end men looked for cometh not,
And a path is there where no man thought:
      So hath it fallen here.

Made in the USA
Middletown, DE
14 October 2020